Books by David H. C. Read

SONS OF ANAK

I AM PERSUADED

THE CHRISTIAN FAITH

THE
PATTERN
OF
CHRIST

David H. C. Read

THE

PATTERN

OF

CHRIST

CHARLES SCRIBNER'S SONS · New York

To: GEORGE C. HOOD
FRANK GREBE
MONTAGUE WHITE
ANDREW HAMZA
WILLIAM McQUOID

partners in service

CONTENTS

🎕 INTRODUCTION

The sayings of Jesus Christ known as the Beatitudes are part of the spiritual heritage of the world.
They are embedded in our literary as well as religious tradition. They are familiar to millions who
know little else of the content of the New Testament. They form the opening statement of the
"Sermon on the Mount" by which many of our
contemporaries claim to live.

Yet all who have taken the trouble to examine
these pronouncements that begin "Blessed are
. . ." will confess that they are by no means obvious and acceptable moral truths. Nothing could be
more remote from the religious platitudes that
normally find currency in our world. Therefore
each generation has to reckon with them afresh

and try to hear what these surprising words may mean in contemporary terms.

It is this writer's conviction that they cannot be understood without the framework of the total Gospel in which they are set. That is to say that we need to be confronted by Jesus Christ himself—the crucified and risen Lord—if we are to know what this good life is of which he speaks. This does not mean that the Beatitudes are meaningless to those who are not convinced Christians. But it does mean that their true power and beauty are revealed, like the stained-glass window, from inside the church, within the family of faith.

This book contains studies of six of the sayings taken from the fifth chapter of St. Matthew's Gospel, with another compelling Beatitude from the twentieth chapter of the Fourth Gospel. It is offered with the prayer that a renewed hearing of these revolutionary words in our own revolutionary age may lead us all closer to that way of life that I have called the Pattern of Christ. The translation throughout is that of the King James Bible unless specified N.E.B. for the New English Bible, or R.S.V. for the Revised Standard Version.

David H. C. Read,
Madison Avenue Presbyterian Church, New York City

THE
PATTERN
OF
CHRIST

HAPPY ARE THE GOD-HUNGRY

 BLESSED *are they which do hunger and thirst, after righteousness: for they shall be filled.*

MATTHEW 5:6

A young couple are coming out of the church. They have just been married. As they pause for a moment on the steps they look each other in the eyes, and for a moment the world stands still. In the crowd around them someone murmurs: "How happy they are!"

A surgeon has just been called out at night for an emergency operation. He works with all his skill and speed and at the end he is sure that a life has been saved. When he arrives home at last exhausted his wife sees past the weariness and says to herself: "How happy he is!"

An old woman steps off the gangway at the Port of New York. A little family is waiting on the dock,

13

and there is the son she has not seen for twenty years. Tears are running down her cheeks, but everyone around would say: "How happy she is!"

These are our beatitudes. When we say this we are expressing a spontaneous opinion of what happiness means. Our beatitudes tell a good deal about what we think the good life is. They range from mere exclamations of envy at someone's good fortune to something like a revelation of God, a sudden vision in which we understand what the Bible means by "blessedness." At the lowest level we're just venting our congratulations tinged with jealousy. As the old song puts it:

> *O lucky Jim!*
> *How I envy him!*

At a higher level we glimpse, as in the little scenes I have just painted, a picture of what fulfilment and satisfaction can mean. At the highest level of all we begin to understand something of the eternal satisfactions that God has designed for us, the kind of fulfilment foreshadowed by the words: "Eye hath not seen, nor ear heard, neither have entered into the heart of man, the things which God hath prepared for them that love him." And then we say: "How blessed!"

Is there anyone whose judgment we would rather have on what makes for true human happiness than Jesus Christ? When he looks out on the crowds of ordinary men and women, whether on a hillside in Galilee or on the streets of New York City in a rush hour, who are the people whom he singles out for this: "How happy! How blessed!"? That's what I want to know, and what I believe you want to know. For it is Christ's pattern of the good life that we seek—the kind of life that he thought truly happy and fulfilled, the kind of life that we have seen in him. Listen to his voice again, trying to let each one of these highly-charged verses we call the Beatitudes explode with fresh meaning in our minds and hearts.

"Blessed are they which do hunger and thirst after righteousness: for they shall be filled." The key word is "righteousness" and we are handicapped right away by not knowing what it means. Ask someone today to paint a verbal portrait of a "righteous" man and the chances are that the result would be strikingly similar to the Pharisee in the parable, the man who said that he was not an extortioner, or unjust, or an adulterer; that he fasted twice a week, and was a faithful tither. Isn't that righteous? Surely performing one's religious duties is right, and being greedy, dishonest, and licentious is wrong? Then why did Jesus say that it was the other man in the story who "went down to his house justified" (i.e., "made righteous") rather than the other?

We'll clearly have to expand our understanding of what he means by "righteousness." Surely it does include these virtues of the honest and religious man. Jesus is certainly not saying that we have to scrap the morality of the Ten Commandments. What he did say was: "Except your righteousness *exceed* the righteousness of the scribes and Pharisees, ye shall in no case enter into the kingdom of heaven." It is not something less than Pharisee-morality he is talking about but something more— the extension of the outward obedience of the act to the inward obedience of the thought, the extra mile traveled beyond the requirement of the law, the spontaneous act of love that overflows when justice has already been done.

So the portrait has to be corrected. The honesty, the duty-doing, the purity is still there; but there is something more. The figure of the grim and stern-faced Puritan begins to recede and another image comes gradually to view. Righteousness begins to look more and more like a portrait of Jesus Christ himself. What we call morality is still there— honesty, purity, fidelity to the highest degree—but it is rounded out, fulfilled, made alive, we might even say "humanized" by the outflowing of a stupendous and spontaneous love. As we watch righteousness being clothed in the flesh and blood of Christ it ceases to be a cold and stern ideal and begins to exert the attraction of the infinitely desirable. Righteousness moves out of the frozen wisdom of the Book of Proverbs into the neighboring poetry of the Song of Songs. "Draw me, we will run after thee: the king hath brought me into his chambers . . . he brought me to the banqueting house, and his banner over me was love." [SONG OF SOLOMON 1:4; 2:4]

But lest we think that this fascinating word can be dissolved into a romantic yearning after the spiritual beauty of Christ we must listen also to its practical overtones. For the Beatitude is given this translation in the New English Bible: "How blest are those who hunger and thirst to see right prevail." The love that fills the righteousness of Christ is not simply a virtue to be desired and worshipped. It is a passion for justice. The "fairest Lord Jesus" of one hymn is the same as the Son of God "who goes forth to war" in another. The blessing of the Lord is called upon those for whom righteousness is not a private virtue to be cultivated but a campaign to be waged on behalf of others. To hunger and thirst after righteousness is to be restless and dissatisfied so long as there is injustice around us to be rectified, manifest wrongs to be set right. When you hear the words "civil rights" do you not catch an echo of this text? Whatever our views on methods and policies for achieving justice, we have to listen to the question: Am I really hungering and thirsting that all my fellowmen may enjoy the rights and liberties to which they are entitled? The righteousness that Jesus commends is not a possession but a passion, and its source and inspiration is not in us but in God.

Now we can see why our Lord lays the emphasis on those who hunger and thirst. If he had said, "Blessed are the righteous," everyone would have understood. That's what moralists have been saying in every generation. "If you're good, you'll be happy." The crowd around him on the Mount would have expected him to say just that. The Psalms, for instance, are full of such statements. The first verse of the first psalm reads: "Blessed is the man that walketh not in the counsel of the ungodly, nor standeth in the way of sinners, nor sitteth in the seat of the scornful." "Blessed are the righteous" is what we are told by the law and the prophets. But this is not what Jesus said. And thank God that he didn't. For there is no gospel in

such a word. It's not good news to people like us
who know how far we are from the righteousness
we see in Christ, who know how little we have
done to set right the wrongs around us, to be told
that the righteous are happy. It is entirely different
when we hear what Jesus actually said: "Blessed
are they which do hunger and thirst after righteousness; for they shall be filled."

In the light of this Beatitude we can understand
the behavior of Jesus which was so shocking to the
religious leaders of his day. They expected a teacher of righteousness to go around commending the
upright and the devout, to associate with the moral
elite, saying, Blessed are the righteous; and adding,
with a stern glance at the notorious sinners of his
day, Cursed are the unrighteous. Instead they
found him mixing with everybody on an equal
basis, even sometimes seeking out the most dis-
reputable people—the rogues, the outcasts, the cor-
rupt officials, the prostitutes, the panhandlers. And
his word to everybody was, "Blessed are they which
do seek after righteousness." We entirely misun-
derstand what he is saying if we think that he was
commending the immoral way of life; that he
actually preferred the dishonest to the honest, the
impure to the pure, the rogues to the respectable.
He was simply saying by word and action that what

matters above all is the inner direction of the heart and mind. What he looked for was not the moral achievement, but the moral desire; not the sense of 'having arrived' religiously, but wanting to be on the way; not the claim to possess God, but to hunger after him.

Look again at the Pharisee and the Publican at prayer. We should see them as individuals, not as representatives of a category or class. In no sense is our Lord indicating that it's better to be a dishonest and greedy tax collector given to adultery than an upright churchman who seeks to fulfil his moral and religious obligations. He simply gives us these two men, and lets us see into their souls. "The Pharisee stood and prayed thus with himself [apparently not with God—have you ever done that?], God, I thank thee that I am not as other men are. . . ." [LUKE 8:11] In this man, for all his public virtues, there was not the slightest trace of a hunger and thirst after righteousness. He was sure he already had it. "And the Publican, standing afar off, would not lift up so much as his eyes unto heaven, but smote upon his breast, saying, God be merciful to me a sinner." [LUKE 8:13] This man, for all his notorious vices, had in him at this moment the one thing that mattered—a thirst for righteousness, a hunger for God. He was a scoundrel, but at the point of this prayer he knew it, confessed it, and desired with all his heart the mercy of God.

"Happy are the God-hungry," says Jesus, "for they shall be satisfied." And that, you know, is the gospel. While we were yet sinners—not when we had attained righteousness—Christ died for us. [ROMANS 5:8] " I came," said Jesus, "not to call the righteous, but sinners to repentance." This is what St. Paul means by these difficult statements about the righteousness of God being revealed to us, conferred on us, imputed to us. It is when we acknowledge that we are not righteous, and when we desire above all else the righteousness of God that we shall be filled.

People sometimes ask us ministers if we think they are suitable persons to become church members, or if they are really entitled to participate in the Holy Communion. Apparently there is still an idea abroad that certain moral requirements, a level of righteousness, are required. The only answer a minister is empowered to make is that the one requirement is the honest desire for God, a genuine hunger after the good life he has revealed in Christ. Christ did not found his church for those who were already satisfied, but for those who were

not. He does not welcome to the Sacrament of his
Body and Blood those who are sure they are good
enough, but those who know they are not.

But conscious of our need, we might let this
word of Jesus penetrate this farther. I may be quite
willing to admit that I am not righteous, that I am
a very long way from the stature of Christ, that I
have not done much to promote justice and mercy
in our world. But do I really hunger and thirst
after these things? These are strong words, you
know. When you are really hungry food becomes
an absolute obsession. When thirst has gripped you
the thought of water is a constant mirage before
your eyes. What Jesus asks us here is, How deeply
do you desire what I have to offer? How hungry are
you for God? How serious are you about working
for his justice? How concerned are you about the
good life he wants for all his children?

For a feeble desire for God little or nothing is
promised. But the hungry and thirsty will be filled.
That's another good strong word. "Foddered" was
what Jesus said, indicating the full satisfaction of
our needs. It is not our goodness but our desire for
it to which he responds. And he responds according
to the strength of our desire. That is what he looks
for as we present ourselves at his Holy Table. He
looks through the successes and the failures, the

virtues and the vices, the gains and the lapses, the joys and the sorrows that are represented here, and he asks if we really want what he has to offer—his righteousness, his life poured out for us. And if we do he has for us the blessing and the promise. "Take ye, eat ye . . . drink ye, all, of this." "Blessed are they which do hunger and thirst after righteousness: for they shall be filled."

THE HAPPINESS OF THE HUMBLE

 BLESSED *are the meek:*
for they shall inherit the earth.
MATTHEW 5:5

"It isn't true." That is the instinctive, honest reaction of nearly all of us to this saying of Jesus, taken as it stands.

Happy are the meek? In the pursuit of happiness, which the Declaration of Independence holds to be one of our inalienable rights, the meek are surely among the casualties rather than the winners. Happiness is the prize of the strong, the tough, the successful, the men and women who know how to get what they want. Look at the smiling people who beam at us from the advertisements, rejoicing in the acquisition of a new car or refrigerator or the discovery of the perfect cigarette, or attending the church of their choice. They all look very happy but none of them looks meek.

24

The meek man is that poor fellow in the "before-and-after" stories who gets pushed around on the beach, who gets nowhere with the girls until he takes the muscle-building course. Is he happy? Has anyone really the desire to be known as meek? Would you want to be part of a meek institution, a meek business, or to have your nation considered meek in the councils of the world? Miserable are the meek, we would say, for they get trampled on. In a society where we admire the man of decision who can impose his will, the person with determination to achieve success and with the qualities of drive, energy, and leadership, meekness begins to look almost like an un-American activity.

With such a picture of the meek in our minds we are astonished at the audacity of the reason our Lord gives for their happiness. "For they shall inherit the earth." The first Beatitude, which I take to be almost a double of this one ("Blessed are the poor in spirit") at least gives a different reason— "for theirs is the kingdom of heaven." Now, that we can begin to understand. Their happiness, we think, is to be postponed. Perhaps they have a miserable time here, but in the beyond they will have their reward. We may not believe it, but we can accept the possibility that in heaven some of these meek people will have a better deal. But this

Beatitude says something quite different: "Blessed are the meek: for they shall inherit the earth." Their reward is right here and now.

Since none of us would be prepared to say that Jesus Christ said something that is plainly not true, we have to decide what to do with this text. With a little scholarly help we might succeed in getting rid of it altogether. It's not in St. Luke's list of Beatitudes; in the manuscripts of St. Matthew its position varies as though it were a kind of scribal afterthought; and in any case it is a direct quote from Psalm 37:11, where we read, "The meek shall inherit the earth." But even the few who might have the skill to operate on the text in this way, and the nerve to decide that Jesus never said it, are still faced with the fact that what it says is consistent with all the rest of the Beatitudes, and with the entire life and teaching of our Lord and his apostles. The average reader, however much he wants to object to the saying, recognizes it as the authentic voice of Jesus. So we have to try other methods of softening its impact.

The most popular of these is to say that this is a counsel of perfection that applies to a strictly limited group of people. In the medieval church it was taught that the heroic moral code of the Sermon on the Mount applied to those who had ac-

cepted the call to a monastic life. They were the
ones who were majoring in Christianity: the rest
could be content with a less strenuous ethic. So
perhaps it was true that in the monastery or the
convent the meek inherited the earth. Ideally in
such a community the humblest member should be
held in the greatest honor, and elected to the position of leadership. Protestants rejected this double
standard in theory but have often restored it prac-
tically in another form. The church member working in business or industry may be inclined to say:
"This 'happy are the humble' talk makes no sense
in the circles in which I move to earn my living,
but it probably works out for those who are isolated from the rough-and-tumble—ministers, for
instance." I remember once being told in a Scottish
church that a certain young man was going to
enter the ministry. "I'm so pleased," said my infor-
mant, "he's just the type—a nice, harmless boy he
always was." Let me tell you that this kind of
wriggling out of the text won't work. For not only
is there no trace in the New Testament of such a
double standard for Christians, there is even less
trace of any such saintly company of clergy—inside
or outside the monastery. Conditions may be different but this text is every bit as challenging to a
minister or a missionary as to the businessman, the

laborer, or the politician. There is no visible human community where the meek are obviously inheriting. The "nice harmless boys" can end up as aggressive and status-conscious clerics. This word applies to all of us—or to none of us.

If we can't eliminate or deflect this word, the only way left to us is to try to discover just whom Jesus has in mind by "the meek." I don't need to tell you that he didn't speak in Elizabethan English from which this word has come sliding downhill to us. The translators then attached no soft and squelchy meaning to the word. You can see that from a familiar Old Testament story. You remember the Hebrew who was brought up in Pharaoh's palace as a prince of Egypt; then identified himself with his own people by laying low a taskmaster who was brutalizing a Hebrew slave; then stood up to the Pharaoh demanding that he let his people go; then led a rag-tailed mob through the desert, welding them into a self-respecting nation in spite of constant bickering and threatening disaster? You remember his immense strength of character, his vigorous leadership, his resounding speeches, his indomitable will? "Now this man Moses," says the King James Bible, "was very *meek*, above all the men which were upon the face of the earth."

So we forget about "meek" in its modern dress.

We now translate the original Greek with the words "humble," "of a gentle spirit," or, "those who claim nothing." Since Jesus was not speaking in Greek we have to guess at the actual Aramaic word he used, and then find its nearest equivalent. Instead of getting bogged down in semantics it is best to take this word "humble" and round it out with the qualities suggested by the kind of humility that Jesus both taught and praised and practiced.

Let's take the word into the home. What does it mean there? When we use the phrase, "He came from a humble home," we often imply that a man has done pretty well for himself, and the last place he's likely to get back to is the "humble home." But we know better than that. It's not the scarcity of the furnishings nor the limited accommodation that makes a humble home. It's the spirit within. I've been in humble homes in every class of society —from the cottage to the palace. (It might be humbler not to mention the palace.) Humility is at work in a home where this admonition from the marriage service of our Church is being fulfilled: "He has instructed those who enter into this relation to cherish a mutual esteem and love; to bear with each other's infirmities and weaknesses; to comfort each other in sickness, trouble, and sorrow. . . ." In the humble home there is discipline without domineering, freedom with respect for another's freedom, love without possessiveness; there is a gentleness in judgment, a considerateness in little things, a courtesy that flows from constant thought for others. We know at once what Jesus meant when we picture the home where this humility is lacking, the home torn apart with conflicting egos, where husband and wife, parents and children, are only concerned with asserting their rights and getting their way. In one form or another pride is the homewrecker. Since none of our homes is perfectly humble, and since the instability of the home is a major problem of our day, is there any word more relevant and understandable than this: "Happy are the humble; for they shall inherit the home"?

Let's take the word out into the world where there's work to be done, all kinds of people to deal with, and ambitions to be fulfilled. Does humility really mean happiness in the affairs and encounters of everyday? If we think of humility in terms of weakness and subservience, of self-depreciation and constant surrender to the opinions and decisions of others, then it certainly does not. But there is no word in the New Testament to indicate that this was the kind of humility that our Lord either commended or practiced. He didn't choose a set of "yes-men" as his disciples, nor did he send them out to grapple with the world, the flesh, and the devil with soft words and innocuous actions. It wasn't "gentle Jesus meek and mild" who flayed the hypocrites with burning words, who referred to King Herod as "that fox," who cleared the courts of the temple single-handed, and who stood up to the Roman governor with the dignity of a majestic silence.

The humility of Christ is consistent with strength of character, with recognition of one's abilities, with decisive action, and with legitimate ambition. In fact it is the foundation for their true exercise. What it is not consistent with is sheer self-sufficiency, the desire to impose our own will at all costs, and the refusal to learn from others. It is not consistent with the burning desire always to be recognized and appreciated, a hypersensitivity to our own status and rights. True humility is to be found in people of all temperaments and rank in society. The centurion who came to Jesus asking for the healing of his servant is a vivid example of humility in action. I cannot imagine that a high-ranking officer in the Roman army would be described by any of his soldiers as "meek" in our sense of the word. He was completely conscious of his authority and ability. "I say to this man, Go, and he goeth: and to another, Come, and he cometh: and to my servant, Do this, and he doeth it." Yet look at the implications of the story. There was a deep humility in this man. First he was humble enough to be concerned about his servant's health. It would have been easy enough to get rid of him and find a fit replacement. To be humble is to open to the needs of others, no matter who they are. Then, secondly, he had the amazing humility to recognize in Jesus an authority in the spiritual world. Another Roman officer with equal rank and ability might very well have scorned the idea of approaching a young Jewish teacher with this kind of request, unless it was a rough command to do what he could. When the British occupied India there were soldiers who knew how to respect representatives of ancient wisdom and religion—and those who did not. The truly great among them had this humility. Listen again to the Roman face to face with a native of this occupied territory. "Lord, I am not worthy that thou shouldest come under my roof: but speak the word only, and my servant shall be healed." This is the humility that inherits the earth, the humility that acknowledges goodness and spiritual power wherever it may be found, the humility that opens doors to a fuller and richer life.

The picture begins to grow within us of the humble man in the image of Jesus Christ. Strong, courteous, considerate, reverent—truly gentle, in the sense in which we speak of a "gentleman." He inherits the earth, for this is the key to a sovereign freedom in our relationships. The arrogant, the self-seeking, the status-conscious, the conceited shut themselves off from the treasures of the world of human relationships. The really humble have a freedom and gaiety that our word "meek" does nothing to suggest, but that comes out well in the French version: *Heureux les débonnaires!*

We could trace this truth through every avenue of human experience. Take the word into the laboratory where the scientist is conducting his research. The man who is encrusted with his own theories, arrogantly determined to prove himself right at all costs, shuts himself off from the world of true discovery. But the man who is humble enough to let nature talk to him, who modifies his theories in the light of emerging fact, who is teachable by both nature and his colleagues, he is the one who inherits the earth, the one to whom nature yields her secrets.

Take the word into the adventure of the mind, the arena of discussion and debate. The humble have their convictions, profound and strong. But they hold their minds open to new truth wherever it may come from. They do not imagine that they possess infallible wisdom but are ready to heed Oliver Cromwell's injunction to "conceive it possible you may be mistaken." Take the word into the poet's study, the artist's studio, the concert hall. Is there not in the greatest of the artists a humility, a receptiveness to what nature and a human nature reveals, that makes them inherit the beauty of the earth? Isn't this what Wordsworth called:

> *that blessed mood,*
> *In which the burthen of the mystery,*
> *In which the heavy and the weary weight*
> *Of all this unintelligible world*
> *Is lightened . . .*
> *While with an eye made quiet by the power*
> *Of harmony, and the deep power of joy,*
> *We see into the life of things.*
>
> TINTERN ABBEY

So we come to the deepest meaning of this humility, that is the pattern of Christ. Bring this word to that central place where we seek the ultimate meaning of our lives, where we want to know if there is a God, where we search for the faith of which the Bible speaks, where we struggle to know and live the Christian life. In the approach to all the great questions of religion the keyword is humility. This does not mean that we simply abandon our own processes of thought and say: "Tell me what to believe and I'll believe it." But it does mean that we have to abandon our claim to be self-sufficient, to be our own god, to control and run our lives in absolute autonomy.

The one great obstacle to a living faith, and to our growth in Christian understanding and character, is pride. In the Genesis story Adam inherits the earth. "And God said, Let us make man in our image, after our likeness: and let them have dominion over the fish of the sea, and over the fowl of the air, and over the cattle, and over all the earth . . ." Then pride comes in, the pride that refused the one condition of inheritance—respect and reverence for the Creator-God. Adam wants to be his own master, to live without his God. And he finds himself outside in the wilderness with a flaming sword barring the return to paradise.

This is our story. It is still pride that keeps us from our inheritance. Here we are, with the most amazing opportunity ever offered for the conquest of hunger, disease, illiteracy, war, and other scourges of mankind—and yet troubled on every side, despairing, poised on the brink of destruction. Why? Because pride is still at work; pride of intellect that will not hear God's word, pride of possession that makes for greed, pride of race that makes for hatred and violence, pride of heart that seals one person off from another. Do we not need to hear the voice that says: Happy are the humble; for they shall inherit the earth?

In such a world the church must still declare that God has not left us alone in our pride. He sent his Son. And how did he come? What was this revelation to which we are called to respond? A demonstration of the power and authority of the Lord our God? Let me simply flash one picture before your eyes. It is a little room in Jerusalem, where a group of men are gathered for a meal: this is what we read: "Jesus knowing that the Father had given all things into his hands, and that he was come from God, and went to God; he riseth from supper, and laid aside his garments; and took a towel, and girded himself. After that he poureth water into a basin, and began to wash the disciples' feet . . ." [JOHN 13:3–5]

This man: this God: this action. Now we hear in a new way the ancient words: "Blessed are the meek: for they shall inherit the earth," and we are ready to listen to these searching words: "Let your bearing towards one another arise out of your life in Christ Jesus. For the divine nature was his from the first: yet he did not think to snatch equality with God, but made himself nothing, assuming the nature of a slave. Bearing the human likeness, revealed in human shape, he humbled himself, and in obedience accepted even death—death on a cross. Therefore God raised him to the heights and bestowed on him the name above all names, that at the name of Jesus every knee should bow—and every tongue confess, 'Jesus Christ is Lord,' to the glory of God the Father." [PHILIPPIANS 2:2–8, N.E.B.]

THE PEACEMAKERS

 BLESSED *are the peacemakers:*
for they shall be called the
children of God.

MATTHEW 5:9

I have thought about this sentence many times and
confess that I find it anything but peaceful. It is
one of the most disturbing sentences that Jesus
ever spoke.

It sounds so soft and quiet, especially when we
wrap it up in the beautiful hymn of Whittier,
"Dear Lord and Father of Mankind":

> *Drop thy still dews of quietness,*
> *Till all our strivings cease . . .*

This inner peace is what we all want, and what is
most certainly promised in the gospel. "Peace I
leave with you, my peace I give unto you." So we
search for that peace. But if we think that the

peace of which the Bible speaks is a soothing syrup of the soul to be taken once a week as directed we are most terribly mistaken. If we think it is the kind of peace that is so often offered by the world, a peace that soothes us through forgetfulness, the peace of a temporary euphoria, the peace of the second martini, then we have not heard Christ speak. "Not as the world giveth, give I unto you." The tranquilizers of the world are easily understood; but the peace of God that blesses us "passeth all understanding." For it comes through struggle; it comes through pain. It is the gift of the risen Christ in whose hands are still the marks of the nails. As Studdert Kennedy put it:

Peace does not mean the end of all our striving,
Joy does not mean the drying of our tears;
Peace is the power that comes to souls arriving
Up to the light where God himself appears.

RHYMES, "THE SUFFERING GOD"

In other words there is no quick way to this peace of God, just as there is no shortcut from here to Easter that bypasses Gethsemane and Calvary. There is a cost. The blessedness of peace is for the peacemakers.

Peace*makers*—that is the disturbing word. "Blessed are the peaceful, the peaceable"—that

would be quite simple. People of a peaceful dispo-
sition are usually happy. "Blessed are the peace-
lovers"—that seemed all right until modern double-
talk made "peace-loving" a highly suspect adjec-
tive. But the word is not passive; it is active. Blessed
are the peace*makers*. There is a job to be done.
This kind of happiness cannot be attained by lis-
tening to and reading soothing words. It comes as
we respond, in our daily life, to the call of Christ to
make peace.

In a time of acute conflict—nation against nation, race against race, generation against generation, strife in the home, in the streets, in the
schools, in industry—people as never before long
for peace. The churches pray for peace. Everyone
talks peace. But how many of us are really peacemakers? When we pray for peace, are we enlisting
as active servants of peace, or are we like the
harassed mother of a large and squabbling family
who cries, "For goodness' sake give me a little
peace!"? Do we really want to face our responsibili-
ties in a world of conflict, or are we simply seeking
to be left in relative comfort and tranquility? I
find this word of Christ disturbing because it forces
me to face the ugly questions and supplies no easy
answers.

How would you make peace in Vietnam? It

would be nice to forget about it, wouldn't it? It's
far away; let's leave it to the statesmen and the
generals. But in a democracy all that is done in our
name is our business. And who knows how soon in
our world a distant spark may become a conflagra-
tion that engulfs us all? And in the eyes of God a
Vietnamese village is as precious as Manhattan and
a suffering child is a suffering child anywhere on
earth. How do you make peace? There are some
Christians who give the radical answer: refuse to
fight, abandon all arms. But most of us are uncon-
vinced that such a course would make peace. It
could have the exact opposite effect. Quite apart
from such considerations, the peace of which Christ
speaks is something much more than mere absence
of warfare. It is the outcome of justice and freedom
and mercy. A peacemaker has a more positive task
than mere refusal to fight. In the pattern of Christ
the peacemakers are linked with those "who hunger and thirst to see right prevail." I raise this
problem, not because I have any solution to offer,
but because even where we feel most helpless there
is a peace to be sought and found. The least we can
do is to be constantly aware of the urgent demand
of our times to find the means of assuring interna-
tional order and a just and stable peace, and to
reject the temptation to believe that we are at peace

whenever Vietnam or some other point of tension slips into the back columns of our newspaper. The true peacemaker looks beyond the surface explosions to the great unresolved problems of world poverty, hunger, and over-population.

How do we make peace nearer home, in a situation of racial tension and potential violence? Here again the temptation is to seek the blessedness of the peaceful rather than of the peacemaker. It is so much more peaceful to believe that somehow, with a little bit of luck, this situation will just quietly go away. It is peaceful to pull the blanket over our eyes and think. But one real peep over the edge of the blanket will show us a situation on our doorstep that cries out for the attention of the peacemaker. Murder, narcotics addiction, slum housing, crisis in education—and with it all the most colossal public apathy that afflicts us all. Listen to the words of the prophet Jeremiah: "How do ye say, we are wise, and the law of the Lord is with us? Lo, certainly in vain he made it; the pen of the scribes is in vain. . . . For they have healed the hurt of the daughter of my people slightly, saying, Peace, peace; when there is no peace." [JEREMIAH 8:8, 11] Are we the people who are healing slightly, saying, Peace, peace; when there is no peace? "Blessed are

the peacemakers." Do you see why these words
make me uncomfortable?

Let's look at another situation, still closer to
each one of us. Tension and conflict are not just in
the world and in the nation. They are sometimes
in our homes, our businesses, our personal relationships. I am thinking about what modern jargon would call "intra-personal maladjustment"
but what most of us know as a good old-fashioned
row. It's worth noting that the first picture the
Bible gives us of the family of fallen man is the
story of Cain and Abel. The Fall is followed by a
falling out. And that has been the story. There is
no home, no community, no group of people working, playing, or even worshipping together where
there is never any moment of tension, never anything that could be called a row. There are some
people, of course, who enjoy a row: their life
would seem monotonous without some clash of
personality or opinion. But most of us are, or like
to think we are, peaceable people. Again, Jesus
does not say, "Blessed are the peaceable," but
"Blessed are the peacemakers," and there is a big
difference. The temptation of the peaceable is always to withdraw from trouble. As long as we can
we pretend it isn't there. When it's forced on our

attention we try to smooth it over, to "heal slightly." At our best we are the person whose calm may
bring some healing to the tension: at our worst we
are the person who turns his back when the knife is
flashed and refuses to give evidence, or become in
any way involved. But the peacemaker is the one
who is willing to take the consequences of involve-
ment, the one who wants to know the truth, and
the one who gives himself with courage and with
patience to the work of reconciliation. He is the
one that Jesus calls "blessed."

Come nearer home still. There is a question to
be asked that underlies the tensions of the world,
the nation, and of personal relations. Are you at
peace with yourself? How much of the strife in our
world is caused by men and women who are not
really at peace with themselves? Shakespeare de-
scribing the conflicting forces in us at a moment of
great decision says, "the state of man, like to a little
kingdom, suffers then the nature of an insurrection." We all know how often the hostilities that
break out between men are the result of civil war
within. The Bible finds the root cause of our strife
and conflict in the internal insurrection. The
classic description is St. Paul's confession: "I know
that nothing good lodges in me—in my unspiritual
nature, I mean—for though the will to do good is

there, the deed is not. The good which I want to do, I fail to do; but what I do is the wrong which is against my will; and if what I do is against my will, clearly it is no longer I who am the agent, but sin that has its lodging in me." [ROMANS 8:18–20 N.E.B.]

With the mention of sin Paul may lose some of us, for the word is not in our current vocabulary. But without it we cannot understand the pattern of the peacemaker in the mind of Christ. For the basic peace on which all else depends is the peace that comes to the divided heart, the guilty conscience, the self that, whether we know it or not, is at war with God. As in every other aspect of conflict we try to pretend that all is well. The psychologist would say that we repress our guilt feelings. The theologian would say that we refuse to confess our sins. We say, Peace, Peace, where there is no peace. And if we are at times driven to acknowledge that the conflict exists, we strive in all kinds of ways to make our peace with God. We use this expression freely, but the New Testament has little to say about our making peace with God. It tells us of something infinitely more important and magnificently liberating: that God has made peace with us. This is why Christ came—to proclaim and effect our peace with God. "For he is himself our peace," says St. Paul. In the conflict of the soul, in the turmoil of the conscience, in the torment of our guilt, he is the great Peacemaker. It was for this he came with the angel-chorus of "Peace on earth"; it was for this he lived as the healer of the bodies and souls of men; it was for this he died, a living sacrifice, the just for the unjust, to bring us to God. And it was this peace that he bestowed on his disciples when he rose from the grave.

God has made peace with us. Was this an easy peace? Did he shut his eyes to the sin, saying, Peace, peace, when there was no peace? What the Gospel—this good news—discloses is the infinite cost of the divine peacemaking. "While we were yet sinners, Christ died for us." The cross is the measure of this cost to God. And here we reach the dynamic secret of the peacemaker. For the action and the passion of Christ was a divine initiative. It was a breakthrough in the dismal story of sin and guilt and blame and wrong and vengeance and hate, the vicious circle that enslaves mankind. God in Christ says to us all: "I have made peace. I have shared your suffering. I have absorbed your guilt. I have borne your sins. I accept you as you are. Peace be unto you. You are forgiven."

This is no religious fantasy. The moment men and women like us received and accepted this message they knew that there was a new power of peace alive in their world. They didn't hug this experience of the peace of God to themselves as a kind of private satisfaction. They realized that the initiative of the Peacemaker was alive in them, and they saw the tension and conflicts of their day in a new light. There was, for instance, the deep-seated antagonism of Jew and Gentile. This was naturally the first point where the divine initiative went to work. "He himself is our peace," said St. Paul, and then went on immediately: "Gentiles and Jews, he has made the two one, and in his own body of flesh and blood has broken down the enmity that stood like a dividing wall between them. . . . This was his purpose, to reconcile the two in a single body to God through the cross, on which he killed the enmity." [EPHESIANS 2:14–16 N.E.B.] We may not follow all the intricacies of the apostle's thought, but his central point is clear. The peace that Christ brings is not only between our souls and God, but between the warring sections of humanity. The two are one. For we cannot claim to have peace with God so long as we are dividing the world into hostile groups, so long as we refuse to recognize that our neighbor, whatever his nationality or the color of his skin, is one with us in the reconciliation that Christ has made.

The peacemaker, then, in the pattern of Christ, is the one who takes the initiative, who breaks the circle of hostility, who is ready to share the cost of reconciliation. In the simple terms of our little quarrels and conflicts the peacemaker is the one who takes the first step. In the more complex rows in which we may be involved the peacemaker is the one who is willing to share something of the agonies, to seek for truth, to refrain from hasty judgment, and, above all, to *be* the channel of Christ's peace. When the peacemaker is present there is always something new in every situation of human conflict, for the divine initiative is at work.

It is with this hope that we move out into these baffling and daunting problems that confront us in the nation and the world. Whenever we are tempted to pull the blanket over our head again and pray for the storm to pass, Christ thrusts us out, saying, "Blessed are the peacemakers"; and he reminds us that there is still a divine initiative at work for peace. He will not let us close our eyes to the evils that have to be fought before peace can come. He will not let us simply wait for the evil forces to convert themselves to good. We may have some sympathy for the Frenchman, Alphonse Karr, who said: "If we are to abolish the death penalty, I should like to see the first step taken by our friends

the murderers." (. . . *que MM les assassins commencent.*) But, after all, this is not the Christian
way. The divine initiative demands that the first
step be taken by the followers of Christ. (. . . *que
MM* les *Chrétiens commencent.*)

"Blessed are the peacemakers." Yes: it is a disturbing text, but it is also an exhilarating text, for
we know that when we move in any way toward
making peace in the circles where we move, in the
city where we live, in the world that is torn in conflict, we have behind us the power of the divine
Peacemaker who has reconciled the world unto
himself, and we shall be happy to be called his children.

THE QUALITY OF MERCY

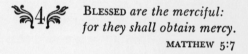 BLESSED *are the merciful:*
for they shall obtain mercy.
MATTHEW 5:7

This looks like the simplest of all the beatitudes, and to the average modern quite the most sensible. The others bother us with their complete reversal of our notions of human happiness. Our idea of success has little to do with meekness and mourning, with being hungry for God, with peacemaking and persecution. The pattern of Christ is flashed before our eyes as a challenge to all that we normally believe. We are asked to turn our thinking upsidedown, and accept the paradoxes of the Kingdom of God. But this, at first sight, makes no such assault upon our minds. "Blessed are the merciful: for they shall obtain mercy." Of course: isn't that what we've always said? "Be decent to others and they'll be decent to you." Millions will go along with that. In fact it could be said to constitute the entire creed of the modern goodhearted man or woman. It makes sense, and it's something you can teach the children.

There is a whole Bible of stories connected with this creed on which we have been raised. Let me remind you of one, a story on which George Bernard Shaw based a famous play. Androcles was a Roman slave who lived in the days of the Emperor Tiberius. He runs away from a cruel master and takes refuge in a cave. A lion comes wandering by limping badly on three paws. He holds out the damaged paw to Androcles who skilfully extracts a huge thorn. Scene Two takes place some time later: poor Androcles is thrown to the wild beasts in the circus, but the lion sent to devour him turns out to be his old friend. So instead of attacking him he nuzzles up and begins to caress him, whereupon the crowd is so astonished that Androcles is set free. Happy ending. Loud cheers. "Blessed are the merciful: for they shall obtain mercy."

This basic plot can be traced in thousands of stories and plays through the centuries, and is still good for many a Hollywood filmscript. If this is what Christ is saying then it would seem very acceptable to the normal kindly and optimistic person. But there has also been a literature of protest

in which the whole proposition has been denied.
From the Book of Job through King Lear to Voltaire and the satirical novelists we find brilliant
minds portraying a world where the merciful do
not find mercy; where the kindly meet with brutal-
ity; where generosity is rewarded with meanness
and contempt. And perhaps, after all, this is the
mood of our day. I can imagine a sick-joke version
of the Androcles story in which we are led through
the whole story to the climactic moment—and then
Androcles is gobbled up, with the explanation that
this was a different lion.

After all, is it really true that merciful people always receive mercy from their fellows? A friend of
mine in Central Europe was engaged in the under-
ground movement against the Nazis. At one point
he was able to save the life of a comrade by hiding
him from the secret police. Some years later, when
the Communists had occupied the country, my
friend was again in opposition and was arrested.
To his surprise he found himself being interro-
gated by the man he had rescued from the Nazis,
now a Communist official. His reward was a merci-
less and implacable spirit and a literal slap in the
face. The hard facts of life teach us that there is no
certainty that goodness will awaken an answering
goodness, that kindness will be met with kindness.

We could all supply examples of ingratitude by which we have been stung, of a complete lack of response to what we felt to be our care and concern. So it begins to look as if, on the one occasion when a beatitude says an apparently obvious and simple thing with which we can agree, both it and we are wrong.

"Blessed are the merciful: for they shall obtain mercy." We have seen how in every instance the ultimate truth of a Beatitude is seen in the experience of Christ himself. His happiness consisted in being humble and hungry for justice, a peacemaker, and pure in heart. It is as we see the pattern of his own life that the inner truth of these paradoxical sayings dawns on us. But how about this one? If anyone was merciful, it was Jesus Christ. Wherever he went the cry went up: "Lord, have mercy upon me," and he never failed to respond. Never has anyone so poured himself out in a ministry of healing, more costly than we can ever understand. He had mercy on the sick in body and in mind; on outcasts to whom no one else would speak; on men and women for whom no one had a good word to say; on children who clamored to be with him when adults wanted to drive them away; on Samaritans and foreigners who crossed his path; on the whole crowd of his contemporaries whom he saw as sheep without a shepherd. His mercy extended far beyond the limits of conventional charity. He sought out the lonely and the despondent. He responded to human need, even when he was told it was against the law of God. This, above all, was a man of mercy. And, what did he receive? A betrayal by one of his friends; a condemnation by religious officials; a flogging by the Roman army; a crown of thorns; and a cross on which he was hoisted amid the jeers and curses of the people he loved. God so loved the world that he gave his Son, and the answer of the world was: "Let him be crucified!"

Surely the real meaning becomes plain. The mercy that the merciful receive is not man's but God's. Blessed are the merciful for they shall receive the mercy of God. It is this truth that is lighted up by the terrible story of Calvary. Behind the cruelty and carelessness of men there is another power at work that responds to this merciful Christ. The waiting and watching Father exerts his recreative love and Jesus Christ is raised from the dead. "Blessed are the merciful for they shall obtain mercy." The most merciful the world has ever known obtains the overwhelming mercy of the Resurrection. This event is written into the Beatitude, as it is written into all the Beatitudes. We understand them in Christ: we experience them in Christ. As St. Peter wrote: "Blessed be the God and Father of our Lord Jesus Christ! By his great mercy we have been born anew to a living hope through the resurrection of Jesus Christ from the dead. . . ." [I PETER 1:3. R.S.V.]

What does this mercy of God mean for us? It would seem right to say in the light of the New Testament that as we share in the mercifulness of Christ we shall share in his resurrection. Happy are the merciful for they shall obtain the crowning mercy of everlasting life. You cannot blot out of the sayings of Jesus the radiant backdrop of eternity. In his day, as in ours, there were many to whom life beyond the grave was inconceivable and talk of resurrection absurd. The astonishing thing about what Jesus said was his implicit trust that God has a destiny for us beyond mortality. He seldom discussed it. He refused to give any detail about it. He simply assumed it. And if we refuse to concede the possibility we cannot truly hear what he is saying on any subject at all. The merciful, he is telling us, may not always find mercy at the hands of men; the kind and good may not always meet kindness and goodness in their way through life; but at the end the mercy of God will dawn upon them like the rising sun and they will be at home in the radiance of the eternal Kingdom.

Is this all that can be said about the mercy of God that is promised to the merciful? For some it is already too much. It sounds like some of that pie in the sky bye-and-bye, if we're nice, good, merciful people here and now. For others it's not enough. They believe in the future life but want some mercy in our present situation—and they are quite right. The mercy of God is not just a distant hope. It is a present reality. It is a help and strength. It is a basis for living, new every morning. It is a restoring power. It is all this—and heaven too.

Do you think my friend who was rebuffed by the man whose life he had saved simply said to himself: "Ah, well; in heaven it will all come out right."? I believe that then and there he experienced the mercy of God, a mercy that sustained him through the whole experience and enriched his life from that day on. The whole difference between the Christian's response to the disappointments, injustices, and slaps in the face that we receive and that of the cynic and the satirist is that instead of turning sour and bitter he finds the mercy of God and grows thereby. The happiness of the merciful depends neither on receiving a reciprocal mercy from men, nor on some distant recompense in heaven, but on the experience of being in harmony with the being of God himself, and with the mind of Christ his son.

The merciful man: the merciful God. We have forgotten what an immense power this co-relation has wielded in our world. The pattern of Christ has been dimmed and confused in the course of Christian history, so that we miss the exhilarating sense of discovery with which it dawned on a tired and sick society. The early Church was a group of ordinary men and women who had learned the quality of mercy in the company of their God. It became all-important in their lives because it was the reflection of what they had discovered about God's attitude to them. Some of this joy and energy has gone out of us because over the years we have come to take for granted both man's mercy and God's.

We suppose that there is a common, almost innate, conviction that it is good to be merciful; to take care of the needy, to be ready to forgive, to be charitable in our judgments, to have compassion on the unfortunate. We forget that the prevailing philosophies in Jesus' world denied the value of mercy, and exalted the ruthless and the strong. Outside the Christian faith it is by no means generally accepted that pity and compassion are qualities to be practiced and admired. From the first to the twentieth centuries the Christian way of life has been openly attacked as a "slave morality," and under the surface of any modern society there are currents of opinion that despise the quality of mercy and favor the hard, the ruthless, and tough. Mercy has little place in the ideologies of extremism wherever they are found. Destroy our Bibles, close all churches, eliminate the pattern of Christ, and how much longer do you suppose mercy and compassion would operate in our explosive world?

If the quality of mercy is a much more precarious possession of the human heart than we commonly think, may it not be because we have also come to take for granted the mercy of God? "Blessed are the merciful: for they shall obtain mercy." How much are we honestly concerned today about obtaining the mercy of God? Wouldn't it be true to say that the ninety-six per cent of the population who profess to believe in God normally take his mercy for granted? Perhaps the biggest difference between us and Christians of past generations is just this—that we have ceased to be surprised at the mercy of God.

> *When all thy mercies, O my God,*
> *My rising soul surveys,*

*Transported with the view, I'm lost
In wonder, love, and praise.*

Thus wrote the sophisticated Addison in the eighteenth century. Is this really how we feel, or are we closer to the spirit of Voltaire who, when urged to seek the mercy of God on his deathbed, is reputed to have replied: "God? Forgive? That's his job." We are a long way from Martin Luther with his passionate cry: "How can I reach a merciful God!" Yet, just as we have settled into this comfortable assumption that God's mercy can be taken for granted, other fears have stirred in the modern soul. The God whose mercy has become an axiom for our thinking seems to withdraw farther and farther from the scene and in his place come the dark powers of nihilism and despair, and our lives are threatened by the meaningless and the absurd. It is these powers that breed a new hardness of heart, a new mercilessness, a new cruelty in the modern world.

The quality of mercy in our lives depends on a profound sense of the wonder and reality of God's mercy—a mercy that is not some vague and abstract quality that ignores the sins and the sufferings of our human lot, but a mercy that breaks miraculously through the tangles of our fears and hates, a compassion that overcomes the alienation of our souls, a love that reaches right down to the point of our despair and accepts us as we are. There is nothing self-evident about the mercy of God as Christ brings it to our world. It is a mercy that breaks into the life of a man or a woman like a divine revolution. "Your sins are forgiven: rise up and walk!" This word was not broadcast from the temple tower so that everyone within earshot was healed and restored in body and soul by the automatic mercy of God. "He that hath ears to hear, let him hear." There had to be an individual response. And how terribly plain he makes it that a man may miss the mercy of God. Can we close our eyes to the stories he told of those who shut themselves off from the mercy of God? Who were they? There was the rich man in the parable who ended up in hell —because there was no compassion in his heart for the beggar at the gate. There was the proud Pharisee who missed the mercy of God—because he had no concern for the publican beside him beyond using him as a contrast to his own virtues. There was the man who lost the great mercy he had received when his debts were forgiven— because he ruthlessly demanded the repayment of an infinitely smaller sum owed by a fellow servant. And, most terribly judged of all, were those who heard the words: "Depart from me ye cursed . . ." —and why? "For I was an hungered, and ye gave

me no meat: I was thirsty, and ye gave me no
drink: I was a stranger, and ye took me not in:
naked and ye clothed me not: sick, and in prison,
and ye visited me not . . . Lord when saw we thee
an hungered, or athirst, or a stranger, or naked, or
sick, or in prison, and did not minister unto thee?
. . . Verily I say unto you, Inasmuch as ye did it
not to one of the least of these, ye did it not to me."
[MATTHEW 25:41–45]

Nothing is clearer in the Gospels than this—the
correlation of God's mercy and man's. Not for a
moment is it suggested that we can buy God's
mercy by acts of charity, but it is made abundantly
clear that it is the merciful spirit that knows the
mercy of God. "Blessed are the merciful: for they
shall obtain mercy." He does not say: Do a merciful deed in order to win mercy from God. This is
not an imperative. It is an indicative. This, says
Jesus, is how the Kingdom is. The happy are the
merciful: for they know the secret of God's mercy.
They don't take it for granted. They know it is
lavish, uncritical, personal, undeserved. So they
learn to practice a mercy that is lavish, uncritical,
personal, undeserved. "Not as the world giveth,
give I unto you," said Jesus, and so we slowly learn
to give without thought of reward, without asking
any questions except about human need.

THE PURE IN HEART

 BLESSED *are the pure in heart: for they shall see God.*

MATTHEW 5:8

Anyone who reads through the Beatitudes slowly and thoughtfully is almost bound to feel that with this one we have reached the climax. Every other facet of the pattern of Christ—the hunger for God, humility, peacemaking, the quality of mercy—is included in this one shining phrase: the pure in heart. And every deep yearning of humanity—for the satisfaction of the mind, for the achievement of true goodness, for the apprehension of beauty—is summed up in the simple words: "For they shall see God."

I once heard a distinguished scholar say that the language of the King James Bible is incomprehensible to modern man. If this is true I suspect it is not only because we have difficulties with Elizabethan English, but because we often prefer to hide from the blunt, hard truths of the Bible in the polysyllabic jungle of our modern obscurities. Suppose we translate into the idiom of the day: "Well-adjusted are those who have achieved an integration of personality, for they will experience an extra-sensory relationship of harmony with the ground of their being." We can get comfortably lost in this kind of verbiage. The sturdy monosyllables of the Bible, I believe, can still find us: "Blessed are the pure in heart: for they shall see God." This is why the preacher's prayer must be that his own verbiage does not blunt the word of God which the Bible tells us "is quick and powerful, even to the dividing asunder of soul and spirit, and of the joints and marrow, and is a discerner of the thoughts and intents of the heart." [HEBREWS 4:12]

"They shall see God." This word is addressed to those who want to see God. That includes far more than those who already believe in him. It includes the man who drops into a church in the vague hope that somehow the God in whom he used to believe, or in whom his friends seem to believe, may become real to him. It includes many who have given up the Church altogether but never give up their search for the truth that will throw light on the mystery of life, or the moment of illumination that lets a man see into the heart of things. It includes all genuine agnostics, seekers, people of a serious and enquiring spirit. It excludes only those who are unconcerned. It has nothing to say to the man who has decided there is no God, to the woman who is perfectly satisfied to live without any thought beyond immediate personal concerns. These words have nothing to say to the man or woman who has ceased to have any spiritual ambitions, who is living on the memory of some past encounter with God and is not aware of any need for further search and discovery. The promise of the Beatitude is for those who, whatever their present belief or unbelief may be, honestly desire the vision of God. It applies to those who "hunger and thirst." It is they who will be filled.

There is little doubt that the words: "they shall see God" referred, as Jesus spoke them, to the ultimate goal of humanity. Once again his eye is on the final destiny of human life. None of his words can be understood if we ignore his unyielding belief that what we are and what we do here and now has consequences in a world that is unseen and eternal. In a time when heaven is often relegated to the land of legend, with the Utopias and Fairylands of the past, we have to listen to the quiet

assurance of this most down-to-earth of teachers. It
will not do to say that he simply absorbed the prevailing ideas of his day. For not only did many contemporary Jews, like the Sadducees, deny the possibility of a resurrection-life, but those who did
believe in heaven elaborated all kinds of theories
about it. Jesus did not. There is nothing in the
gospels about pearly gates and streets of gold. Here
is his definition of heaven—the only one he ever
gave: "They shall see God." And this is what his
disciple John wrote on the same subject: "Now are
we the sons of God, and it doth not yet appear
what we shall be: but we know that, when he shall
appear, we shall be like him; *for we shall see him as
he is.*" [1 JOHN 3:2] Even the Book of Revelation,
with all its brilliant imagery, concentrates on this
same end: "The throne of God and of the Lamb
shall be in it: and his servants shall serve him: and
they shall see his face, and his name shall be in
their foreheads." [REVELATION 22:3, 4]

This is the simple and sufficient declaration of
the Christian faith in all ages, and in all its com-
munions. The goal of humanity is the vision of
God. The ultimate meaning of our lives will be
found in him. The purpose behind all the strug-
gles, the confusions, the sufferings, the slow prog-
ress of our hopes, is that in the end we may see God

and in him find the meaning and the satisfaction
and the joy, as in some mysterious way we are made
like him.

But the vision of God is not just this final goal.
It doesn't belong only in that last chapter in Christian theologies that is labelled "Eschatology" or
"Doctrine of the Last Things." The vision of God
is the first thing that happens to a believer. We
may surely talk as truly about the vision of God at
a baptism as at a funeral. I don't profess to know
exactly what our Lord meant by the words he used
about little children—"In heaven their angels do
always behold the face of my Father" [MATTHEW
18:10]—but they suggest that the spirit of an infant
enjoys already the vision of God. As a child grows
he may still retain a capacity for seeing God that
we adults may envy. In the story of the infant Samuel in the temple, that has inspired some of the
greatest artists, we find a reflection of the simple
wisdom of childhood. The call of God comes to this
boy with such clarity and directness that he believes that it must be the old priest speaking. Yet in
the darkness it is to him, and not to the old servant
of God, that the vision is given.

In mature years, and in a modern scientific civilization, what does it mean to see God? We are inclined to think of this as a mystic experience con-

fined to the very few who have remained detached from the rough-and-tumble of ordinary life and relatively innocent in the sophistication of modern society. We think of them as withdrawn from the world, enjoying their vision of God in some private shrine. But surely the man or woman of faith today is the one who sees God in the events of every day, in the crowded life of home or business, in the experience of both joy and sorrow, in the unexpected encounter, and in the drab routine. We don't have to bypass the material world and seek the vision in some cloudy chancel of the spirit. I believe the promise to the pure in heart is that they shall see God right here and now, and see him in people where others see nothing but a problem, in events where others see nothing but perplexity, and in experiences where others see nothing but frustration and despair.

Isn't this the real difference between a life according to the pattern of Christ and a life on the natural level? Both look at the same stream of people that pass us each day—in our homes, in our jobs, in the streets. The one sees simply a mass of human beings; some pleasant, some unpleasant; some good, some bad; some useful, some useless; a few to be chosen as friends; a few to be recognized as enemies; the vast majority just faceless units of our anonymous society. The other, in all this tangle of human contacts, sees God—God in the close relationship of love and friendship, but God also in the difficult person, God in the hostile person, God in the hopeless person, God in the friction as well as the harmony, the image of God reflected even in the blank faces that sway with us in the mechanized rhythm of the subway car.

Both look at a picture on the television screen—there are the marchers, the speakers, the soldiers. Faces flicker in and out of the picture—saintly faces, devilish faces, tired faces, angry faces, scared faces, joyful faces. What are we looking at? One sees simply another trouble-spot on the map of our restless world, and either takes sides or just sighs for an end to it all. The other sees God—God in the plea for justice and freedom, God in the awakened conscience of his people, God in the anguish of difficult decisions, even God in the terrible martyrdom of the meek. For is it not at the heart of the faith to look upon a man hanging helpless on a cross, the victim of an angry mob and a careless people, and to see God?

This leads to the point where the dividing-line is most clearly seen. When suffering strikes, when we—and not someone else—become the victim of accident or malice or what the world calls wretched

luck, then we can either see nothing but evil, darkness, and misery; or, in the most profound way of
all, we may see God. This is no easy vision, no simple solution for any of us. But we have all known
men and women in whom this faith was visible. I
have visited them in hospitals, seen them in their
homes, or in my study. They have given me more
than I could ever give to them. And the unspoken
thought in my heart has been, "Blessed are the
pure in heart; for they shall see God."

This is the vision of God that many are seeking
even though they may not fully realize what their
quest truly is. We want to see God in people
around us, in the events of today, in our own experiences of both joy and sorrow. We want to see
God in those lonely moments when there is silence
in our souls. But how?

Well, what are we hearing from the lips of
Christ? Is it "Blessed are the minds that are able to
prove that God exists"? The Bible tells us to love
God with all our minds; we have to use our intel-
lects in our religious quest; but how mistaken are
we when we think that someone, or some book, is
going to be able to produce the arguments to let us
see God. If the vision of God depended on the ac-
ceptance of a series of logical propositions, then the
brightest minds would have the clearest vision, and

the dimwits would have little hope. But it is quite obvious that the vision of God has been shared in this world on a quite different plan. Some of the greatest minds alive or dead have been believers—and multitudes of the very simplest. The intellect alone can never be the avenue to the vision of God.

What then? "Blessed are the temperamentally religious for they shall have a tremendous *feeling* of God's presence"? Is there any sign in the New Testament that the disciples were all men of strong religious emotions? Are the people we have known who must obviously see God in their daily life all men and women of an excitable, mystical nature? Of course, our emotions are involved in our vision of God: but we do not have to wait for our feelings to be all churned up in some mountain-top experience before we can begin to see him.

Is it then: "Blessed are the righteous, the good, for they shall see God"? Now we are nearer to the true avenue to the vision of God. Religious truth, it has been said, is morally conditioned. That is to say it is much more closely linked with our will for the good life than with our mental or emotional activities. The Fourth Gospel tells us that Jesus once gave this advice to those who were puzzled about matters of doctrine: "If any man will do his [the Father's] will, he shall know of the doctrine."

[JOHN 7:17] The kind of life we are leading is the clue to our knowledge of God—much more than our ability to follow an argument, or experience a deep religious emotion. But this does not mean that we are being told that unless we are really good we can't see God. Jesus you remember, did not say: "Blessed are the righteous," but "Blessed are they that hunger and thirst after righteousness; for they shall be filled."

So what he is saying here is not "Blessed are the pure" as if only those who had reached a certain level of holiness could see God. The "pure in heart" are those, at whatever stage of moral growth, who strip down to the fundamental simplicity of wanting God above all else; those who strike through all the muddled motives of the heart and say "I want what is true and right and good whatever the cost"; those who give up the double-game of pretending to be honest when they are not, to be chaste when they are not, to be unselfish when they are not. To be pure in heart demands a ruthless honesty with ourselves, and a concentration at the very center of our being on the very highest that we know.

With this decision comes the rebirth of the child within us—the child of God who has been imprisoned by the subtleties and sophistications of our divided minds and hearts. God shows us the pattern of his Christ and says: "Is this—or is it not —what you really want?" With the sheer simplicity of an undiluted "Yes" we enter the kingdom of the pure in heart, and more and more in our daily life, with all its perplexities, we shall see God; more and more in the people and events of our day the vision will be ours; until we reach that final dimension of our existence when, as the Bible says, we shall see him face to face.

THE STRENGTH OF THE SENSITIVE

6

BLESSED *are they that mourn: for they shall be comforted.*
MATTHEW 5:4

The Sermon on the Mount is the one part of our Christian heritage that nearly everyone accepts and approves. Those of other faiths often say that it expresses what they themselves believe. Those who dislike all forms of organized religion can be heard to remark: "The religion of the Sermon on the Mount is good enough for me." Agnostics and atheists in their attack on Christian beliefs and practice can usually find a good word to say for at least this extract from the Bible. And lots of church people who are impatient with dogma and creeds are inclined to say: "I wish the minister would just stick to the simple teaching of the Sermon on the Mount." Some have even the idea that if we could chop off this section of our faith it could be the common ground on which all our religions could meet.

We must not deplore the popularity of our Lord's teaching as recorded in these chapters of the Bible, or grudge anyone his share in these immortal words. But we may be allowed to wonder at times how many of those who exalt the Sermon have really read it through, and whether they have reached beneath the beauty of the familiar words to examine their implications. As we have studied each note in this majestic prelude we call the Beatitudes, it has become clear that we are in the presence of the most startling and disturbing and literally upsetting teaching that men have ever heard. We begin to understand everyone wanting to know about "blessedness"—the happy life. I remember seeing an advertisement for one of these books that offers us the secret of a happy and successful life. The appeal was based quite openly on our desire for riches, prestige, the imposition of our own will on others, and yet making everybody like us. Success guaranteed or money back. The Sermon on the Mount opens with a series of ethical salvos that reverse every single one of the values represented in that advertisement. Happiness is declared to belong to the poor in spirit, the mourners, the meek, the hungry for righteousness, the merciful, the pure in heart, the peacemakers, and the persecuted.

As we take each one of these words of Jesus and try to think it through do we not also find that the only way we can begin to understand what is meant is by looking at Christ himself? We need more than the whole gospel story to throw light on these words. We need the entire New Testament to show us who this is who is speaking to us, and how he can make these words alive in our own experience, *and* we need the whole Bible and the life and witness of the church. This Sermon cannot be detached from the total story of God's revelation to us in Christ. This is why I have called this book not "The Secret of Happiness," but "The Pattern of Christ."

"Happy are the sad." Does that make any kind of sense? But this is exactly what Jesus said. What would a normal sceptical modern man, attending the funeral of a friend, really think if he saw a minister get up, look at the sorrowing group of the bereaved family, and say, "Happy are the sad." Yet, again and again I have done just this. Never could I say the words "Blessed are they that mourn" in such circumstances unless behind them we felt the whole weight of the Christian gospel in its fulness, and could offer to those present the pattern of Christ.

"Happy are the sorrowful." It doesn't really become much easier to understand when we complete the sentence: "for they shall be comforted." It is a strange idea of happiness that suggests that we ought first to be miserable in order to experience the pleasure of being consoled. It reminds us of the man who was asked why he kept banging his head against a wall and replied that he did it because it was so pleasant when he stopped. Once again we are forced to go beneath the surface for the meaning: and once again we shall find that it is the person of Christ himself that will light up for us the interior of this Beatitude. They are all, as has been observed, like the stained-glass windows of a church—on the outside, dusty, meaningless, and obscure, but from the inside, where Christ is worshipped, alive and glowing with the rich colors of his grace.

"Blessed are they that mourn; for they shall be comforted." In this, the most paradoxical of all the Beatitudes, the key to understanding is to identify the mourners. Who are they? We cannot take the sting out of the word. In St. Luke the word is even stronger: "Blessed are ye that weep." [LUKE 6:21]

In our tradition weeping is much less common, especially among men, than in other times and places. But whether it is an outward or an inward weeping everyone of us knows sooner or later this terrible sorrow. The shortest verse in our Bible records that at the grave of Lazarus his friend "Jesus wept." There is no harsh Stoicism in the Christian message. We are not forbidden to express our sorrow. The first light begins to break upon this word when we realize that there is a blessedness in the expression of our grief that is denied to those who steel their hearts. There is a terrible isolation about the man or woman who refuses to give way to mourning, who walks dry-eyed through sorrow and tragedy. No one, we say, can get through to them. Can, then, the grace of God get through with the blessedness of his consolation? If we make ourselves insensitive to our own sorrow is it likely that we shall be sensitive when sorrow comes to others?

If, then, we hear the voice of Christ at such a time, saying, All right! go ahead, mourn—and you will be comforted; we have to remember that not all our sorrow will receive this comfort. The question comes: What are you mourning for? There is a difference between the natural anguish that comes with some terrible loss or separation, and the sheer indulgence of self-pity. If genuine sorrow melts the heart and makes us more able to be of help to others in their distress, self-pity robs us of the power to sympathize. The agony of King Saul in the Old Testament story when he saw his kingdom begin to crumble and his friends and family to desert him, is terrible—but it is utterly self-centered. He stares around at his followers and blurts out: "All of you have conspired against me . . . there is none of you that is sorry for me." [1 SAMUEL 22:8] From then on, a prisoner of his self-pity, he reels downhill to the final tragedy. There was another personal agony years later in nearly the same place. In the garden of Gethsemane Jesus saw the outward signs of his kingdom melt away. The crowds that had hung on his words when he preached this Sermon in Galilee were no longer with him. Of his twelve disciples, one had gone off to betray him, eight were hovering on the edge of flight; and the three nearest to him had fallen asleep. Through the darkness he already felt the approach of the brutal power that would inflict on him the hideous pain of crucifixion. Here was the greatest mourning the world has ever seen, as the mighty heart of Christ was broken in blood and sweat and tears. This was his sorrow and it is not sealed off by any stoic curtain of the soul. But there is no self-pity. Can you imagine him saying to his followers, "There is none of you that is sorry for me"? No; his word is: "Enough! Rise up, let us go."

The mourner of whom Christ speaks feels more than the private sorrow that pierces the heart. He is the one who feels the sorrow in another heart, the sorrow that is never far from any of us, especially in a crowded city. The true mourner is the man or woman who is sensitive to the agonies of this world. It hurts to be sensitive, and this is the cost of discipleship with Jesus Christ. Think of what it means to be really sensitive—to the sorrow of the neighbor when mortal illness has struck, to the needs of the stranger taken suddenly ill in the street, to the conditions in which many of our fellow citizens are living, to the victims of racial prejudice, to the terrible things that happen through war and hunger and poverty throughout the world. Everyone builds defenses because he knows the price of sensitivity. It is so much easier to pass by on the other side; so much less costly not to be involved. But Jesus says, "Blessed are they that mourn"—and this is the mourning that he means.

Some of those who first heard him may, like us, have missed the point. They thought, perhaps, he was only talking about mourners at a funeral. In those days at every funeral there were professional mourners—people who were hired to come into the house and wail and weep at so much an hour. We have our own kind of professional mourners—and they are not the ones he called blessed. There is a big difference between being sensitive to the needs of our neighbors, to the evils of our environment, to the weight of human suffering; and being one of these perpetual deplorers of the state of the world, who moan without ceasing about the terrible things they read about in the papers, who groan with indignation about tragedies in their neighborhood or on the other side of the world, but are not really moved by one spark of active compassion. I wonder what kind of mourners our Lord finds today? Sensitive men and women, who are prepared to pay, in at least some measure, the cost of true compassion, or just professional mourners who wag their heads in solemn, and quite comfortable, disapproval of a wicked world?

Wicked? Yes: there is another element in our mourning. Mingled with sorrow is our knowledge that wickedness lies behind much of the suffering in the world. In what way do we mourn the evil that infects our human situation? There is a verse in a popular hymn by Edward Denny which says:

O give us hearts to love like thee!
Like thee, O Lord, to grieve
Far more for others' sin than all
The wrongs that we receive.

This is truly Christian when it means that our mourning should not be for ourselves when we are the victims of injustice, or cruelty, or bitter words, but for the sin that is their cause. But there is real danger in being a little too quick to "grieve for others' sins." There are professional mourners in every land sighing heavily and very devoutly over the sins of their neighbors, but oblivious to the sins that Jesus condemned most strongly—self-right-eousness, judgement of others—that lie much nearer home. The truly sensitive begin their mourning over sin in the quiet of their own confessional. Only then can they feel something of the weight of the sins that are around us, and that great entanglement of sin that throttles the whole human family. Here again there is a cost—for how can a man take lightly, and confess smoothly, either the burden of his own conscience or the vast network of human sin in which we are all implicated?

"Blessed are they that mourn"? Where is the happiness in this sensitivity to suffering and to sin?

Briefly and simply, in the enormous spiritual strength that can flow into the life that is thus open to our God. If we barricade our hearts against the cry of suffering, if we seal our souls off from the confession of sin, then for all our temporary comfort and furtive happiness, we are the prisoners of our own darkness and there is no way out. But the moment we know what it is to mourn—to be sensitive to the needs and sorrows of others, to be sensitive to our own and others' sins—then we are open to the mighty comfort of God. You know what that "comfort" means? It is not a soft and flabby word. The "fort" in it means strength. The New Testament word *comforter* means the *helper*, the strong one who comes along-side. "Blessed are they that mourn: for they shall be comforted." To the sensitive man or woman comes the grace of the Lord Jesus Christ, bringing forgiveness and the power to forgive, understanding and the power to understand, compassion and the power to be compassionate. There comes the love of God with the assurance that it is the final word in all our tumult and conflict. There comes the communion of the Holy Spirit, binding us together in the strengthening family of belief.

Who is this that comes riding to Jerusalem on Palm Sunday morning? Over the crest of the hill the whole city lies sparkling in the sunshine, the nest of houses where joys and sorrows, sickness and health, riches and poverty live side by side, even as they do now. It is a fair city with its temple and its palaces, and its thriving marketplaces. "And when he was come near," we read, "he beheld the city, and wept over it." Here is the greatest mourner the world has ever known. Here is the infinite sensitivity of the Son of God. And what does he do? Does he turn back to the green pastures of Galilee? Does he issue a statement deploring the state of the nation? No: he goes on, in the power of the Spirit, to take to himself the whole burden, to bear our griefs and carry our sorrows.

> *Ride on! Ride on! In majesty!*
> *In lowly pomp ride on to die;*
> *Bow thy meek head to mortal pain,*
> *Then take, O God, thy power, and reign.*
>
> HENRY H. MILMAN

Do you see how it is in him, and with him, and through him, that we can enter into the deepest truth of these amazing words: "Blessed are they that mourn; for they shall be comforted."

AND YET WE BELIEVE

 JESUS *saith unto him, Thomas,*
because thou hast seen me, thou
hast believed: blessed are they that
have not seen, and yet have believed.
JOHN 20:29

Believe in Jesus Christ risen from the dead. That
was the content of the first Christian sermon ever
preached, when according to the book of Acts,
Peter addressed a huge crowd of people in the open
street and told them that "this Jesus has God raised
up, whereof we are all witnesses." And about three
thousand people "gladly received his word," were
baptized and added to the church.

The church began this way and continued this
way. It was a dynamic and contagious belief in
Jesus Christ, crucified and risen from the dead,
that crashed into the sceptical philosophies of
Greece and the totalitarian power of Rome and

turned that world upside down. It has always been belief in the resurrection that has kept the church alive and expanding. It has been proclaimed in times of peace and order, and in times of tumult and war, in primitive societies and in highly cultured societies, in ages of scepticism and ages of faith. Only a handful of men and women claimed to have seen the risen Christ but millions in every age since have rejoiced to be among those who have not seen and yet have believed. This belief today is confronted by a world of technology, automation, cosmonauts, and television.

In this chapter I want to talk about belief in the resurrection—not just as a Christian tradition that shows up once a year, not just as an item in a creed to which we are supposed to give assent, but as a living and recreative power in our lives as the basis of a Christian pattern of living that has both meaning and direction.

Let us look at the incisive words that open the Sermon on the Mount—the sayings that reveal the pattern of Christ and reveal the life that he calls truly happy. Each one of these Beatitudes strikes down a popular modern notion of what makes for happiness and success.

Our word is, Happy are those with the drive to acquire and the passion to succeed. Jesus says:

Happy are those who hunger and thirst for what is right. Our word is, Happy are those who can impose their wills on others. Jesus says: Happy are the humble. Our word is, Happy are those who have peace of mind. Jesus says: Happy are the peace-*makers*. Our word is, Happy are the thick-skinned and the uninvolved. Jesus says: Happy are the merciful. Our word is, Happy are the uninhibited for they shall see life. Jesus says: Happy are the pure in heart for they shall see God. Our word is, Happy are the self-sufficient and the insensitive for they shall feel no pain. Jesus says: Happy are the mourners for they shall be comforted.

The more we ponder Christ's way in this world of ours the surer we are that in the end he is right. But the qualities of which he speaks cannot be isolated from the Gospel that he brings. This life is his life, and it can only be ours as he brings it to us, and lives it in us. We don't become like this by admiring a distant teacher. We are transformed from within by contact with the living Lord. The moral power of the Gospel flows from belief in Jesus Christ, who died for us and rose in victory from the grave. Therefore, there are recorded for us not only the Beatitudes we find at the beginning of the first Gospel, but the crowning Beatitude that comes at the end of the fourth. This is the word that lights the way into the new life in Christ—the great Beatitude of belief: "Blessed are they that have not seen, and yet have believed."

Again, the wisdom of the world is ready to shout down the word of Christ. Our word today is, Blessed are they who believe what they see. Happy is the man who can offer proofs for all his convictions. Blessed is the new world, free from superstition, where we believe in hard facts demonstrated before our eyes. Seeing is believing. We are the people who have seen the atom explode. We have seen a man return from orbiting the earth. We have seen the computer, the new drugs, the television set. The unseen world belongs to the childhood of the race. We are of age. Blessed are those who live boldly in the cold clear light of the age of science. . . .

There is no question about the immense change that has come over our world with the strict application of the scientific method. Almost every area of life now seems to be within range of its instruments. While our ancestors were prepared to believe all kinds of strange stories on the authority of religion, there is almost nothing too fantastic for us to believe on the authority of science. And we cannot pretend that this is the same kind of belief. For science confirms or demolishes our belief with the evidence of things seen. There was a time when a man could live happily in the belief that the moon is made of green cheese, but now we know that it just isn't so. The spectacular achievements of applied science have created an atmosphere in which the average man is tempted to think that there is nothing left to believe but that which can be seen, or perceived, or deduced by the instruments of science. Everything else—including the classic statements of the Christian faith—is "green cheese," a remnant of the old world of superstition.

Several books that I have read recently call upon the church simply to accept this new self-enclosed, secular world, and to reinterpret all our doctrines so that they can be palatable to the man who believes only what he sees. All that we teach about God, about Christ, about salvation is to be expressed in terms of the secular world, with no overtones of the supernatural, of the world unseen. No one can rightly protest any sincere effort to think through Christian doctrine in the light of every modern discovery about the universe, but in the name of the Christian God and the communion of the saints, I protest any attempt to stifle our belief in the divine dimension that lies within, around, and beyond the things that are seen. There is no discovery of modern man, no penetration into the mysteries of nature that can possibly disturb a mature conviction in the reality of things unseen.

Instead of hesitating about our statements of faith we are in a position to declare with a new relevance and conviction our belief in that which lies beyond the limits of the seen. For is it not becoming clearer every day that man's technical mastery of his environment does not in itself lead to his happiness and fulfilment? The more we are able to control the things that are seen the more acute become such questions as, What shall we do with our new powers? or, What kind of world do we want to live in? The more amazing our outreach into space, the more acute becomes the question of meaning and purpose in this bewildering universe. The vistas opened up by the techniques of control of human personality—by drugs, operations on the brain, subliminal influence—demand an answer to the question of what all this is for, what kind of persons we are meant to be. Everyone of these urgent questions—for what? why? what should we do? what is best? where are we going?— can only be answered on the basis of belief in that which is unseen. No one has seen right or wrong. No one has seen goodness. No one has seen love. No one has seen a moral standard. Yet it is our beliefs in these things unseen that will determine the

future of the race. We can believe in the hydrogen
bomb. It belongs to the world of things seen. But
infinitely more important is the belief in things
unseen that animates the man whose finger is on
the button.

The more we think about the condition of the
world today the plainer it is that the man or
woman who is hypnotized by the power of things
seen, who lives in the restricted world of scientifi-
cally proved fact and technical achievement, is not,
after all, the happy one. For us, as for our ancestors, the truth of Christ breaks through:
"Blessed are they who have not seen, and yet have
believed."

Any sensitive person is aware of this in our
quivering world. The artist knows it: the musician
knows it: the dramatist knows it: the statesman
knows it: and, with increasing force the scientist
knows it. Man does not live by bread alone, nor by
any amount of extended control over the material
world. There is something else, something that
escapes the investigation of our instruments and
the controls of our techniques, that matters more.
This is why a generation that is rushing forward at
an ever accelerating speed in the conquest of the
natural world is strangely ready to listen to the
man who talks of the things that are unseen and

eternal—to a Schweitzer, a Hammarskjöld, a Pope John.

"Blessed are they that have not seen, and yet have believed." Does this mean that any old belief will do? Does this imply that the credulous will receive a blessing that is denied to the sceptical? Christ says nothing about a general blessing on those who find it easy to believe, and the reference here is quite specific. There are people who are driven by the pressures of modern life to all kinds of fantastic beliefs in things unseen. It is reported that the Duke of Wellington, the victor of Waterloo, once was accosted by a man on a railway platform who raised his hat and said, "Mr. John Smith, I believe?" "Sir," said the Duke, "if you believe that, you will believe anything." There are people of whose beliefs we feel like saying the same. The blessing of this Beatitude is not for the credulous, or the superstitious. It is for the sane, serious, sensitive man or woman, confronted with the affirmation that Jesus Christ, the Son of God, having died on the cross in this world we know, was seen alive again in that same world, and is alive today.

It's not an easy belief. But it comes to us with the backing of the finest line of witnesses this world has ever known—stretching back through the parents and grandparents, ancestors who lived by this faith in rugged times, reformers who changed the course of history, thinkers whose books molded a civilization, saints whose lives were a mirror of the unseen splendor, martyrs who died in agony rather than deny the living Christ. It comes to us from the very heart of the world unseen as the Word of a God who has shared the agonies, the frustrations, the absurdities of human life. This is no soft doctrine of escape into an unseen world of blissful irresponsibility. It is a story of the Son of God who wrestled with the powers of darkness, who knew the abyss of nothingness that threatens the human soul, who endured the final mockery of death. It tells us that he—this Christ who was crucified and descended into hell—came back victorious, and offers us the key to the world unseen. If it is, as some would say, an absurd story, that is its glory. "I believe," Tertullian, one of the great fathers of the faith, reputedly said, "because it is absurd." He meant, of course, that only this astounding story of the death and resurrection of the Son of God, is vast enough to cover the agonies, the mysteries, and the absurdities of our existence. There is only one affirmation of faith in the unseen that is big enough to meet the real experience of us all—joy and sorrow, sin and sainthood, suffering and ecstasy, life and death—and it is *I believe that Jesus Christ rose from the dead.*

"Blessed are they that have not seen, and yet have believed." "Happy are they that have not seen and yet have believed." We have almost forgotten that this is a happy belief. What heavy weather we make today about our problems of belief. How solemn are the books and speeches that wrestle with the dialogues, the involvements, the commitments of our modern jargon. Can we not, at least on Easter morning, catch again the joyful contagion with which this story burst upon the world? Yes; I know what a troubled world this is, what a network of problems lies in our path, what weighty decisions lie ahead for mankind, what disasters can flood in on us at any time. But I believe in Jesus Christ, the Lord of life and death. In the very heart of the unseen world there is no final disaster, but a victory of love.

Is this just a passing feeling when the Easter crowds are out, the hymns are soaring, and the resurrection trumpets sounding? What about the quiet moment when the tumult and the shouting dies?

Dag Hammarskjöld has an entry in his *Markings* about an Easter evening as he watched a man and his little daughter come in the aftermath of celebration. "He came with his little girl. She wore her best frock. You noticed what good care she took of it. Others noticed too—idly noticed that, last year, it had been the best frock on another little girl. In the morning sun it had been festive. Now most people had gone home. The balloon sellers were counting the day's takings. Even the sun had followed their example, and retired to rest behind a cloud. So the place looked rather bleak and deserted when he came with his little girl to taste the joy of Spring and warm himself in the fresh polished Easter sun. But she was happy. They both were. They learned a humility of which you still have no conception. A humility which never makes comparisons, never rejects what there is for the sake of something 'else' or something 'more.' "

In the quiet of our own homes, in the quiet of our own hearts, we can know that humility as we simply, and gladly accept the presence of the living Christ—not looking for something else, not waiting for something more. Do you want anything else? Do you wait, like Thomas for something more, something tangible, something visible? "Blessed are they that have not seen, and yet have believed." That blessing can be yours.